OPPOSITES

AND A FEW DIFFERENCES

Poems and Drawings
by Richard Wilbur

Harcourt, Inc.
San Diego   New York   London

For Aaron

Copyright © 2000 by Richard Wilbur

Opposites was first published in 1973 by Harcourt, Inc.

More Opposites was first published in 1991 by Harcourt, Inc. Poem numbers
4, 8, 9, 15, 16, 18, 24, and 28 first appeared in *Cricket* magazine in 1990.
Poem numbers 5, 17, 19, and 23 first appeared in *The Formalist* in 1990.

First Harcourt Paperbacks edition 2000

Library of Congress Cataloging-in-Publication Data
Wilbur, Richard, 1921–
Opposites, more opposites, and a few differences/by Richard Wilbur.
p. cm.
Summary: A collection of light-hearted poems
centering around words and their opposites.
1. English language—Synonyms and antonyms—Juvenile poetry.
2. Children's poetry, American. 3. Humorous poetry, American.
[1. English language—Synonyms and antonyms—Poetry.
2. Humorous poetry. 3. American poetry.] I. Title.
PS3545.I32165A6 2000
811'.52—dc21 99-29053
ISBN 0-15-202347-X

A C E G H F D B

Printed in the United States of America

L / MAY 2001

Here are some…

OPPOSITES

1

What is the opposite of *nuts*?
It's *soup!* Let's have no ifs or buts.
In any suitable repast
The soup comes first, the nuts come last.
Or that is what *sane* folks advise;
You're nuts if you think otherwise.

2

What is the opposite of *flying*?
For birds, it would be *just not trying*.

Perhaps the opposite for us
Would be *to take a train or bus*.

3

The opposite of *foot* is what?
A *mountain top*'s one answer, but
If you are thinking of a bed,
The opposite of foot is *head*.
To ancient generals, of course,
The opposite of foot was *horse*.

4

What is the opposite of *cheese*?
For mice, it's *anything you please*.
So fond are they of cheese, that mice
Think nothing else is very nice.

I too like cheese, I must admit.
I'm certainly not opposed to it.

5

The opposite of *junk* is *stuff*
Which someone thinks is good enough,

Or *any vessel on the seas*
That isn't in the least Chinese.

6

What is the opposite of *string*?
It's *gnirts*, which doesn't mean a thing.

7

The opposite of *standing still*
Is *walking up or down a hill,*
Running backwards, creeping, crawling,
Leaping off a cliff and falling,

Turning somersaults in gravel,
Or any other mode of travel.

8

What is the opposite of *riot*?
It's *lots of people keeping quiet.*

9

The opposite of a *hole*'s a *heap*
Just as high as the hole is deep.
How deep's the hole? Go on and measure,
If it will give you any pleasure.

10

What is the opposite of *fox*?
Foxes are clever, while the *ox*,
So we are told, could not be duller:
But is it opposite in color?

The fox is reddish-brown in hue;
Perhaps *a greenish ox* would do.

11

The opposite of *making faces*
Is *not indulging in grimaces,*
Wrinkling your nose, with tongue stuck out,
And rolling both your eyes about.
But letting eyes, and mouth, and nose
Remain entirely in repose.
It's true, however, that a *very*
Fixed expression can be scary.

12

What is the opposite of *two*?
A lonely me, a lonely you.

13

What is the opposite of *doe*?
The answer's *buck*, as you should know.
A buck *is* dough, you say? Well, well,
Clearly you don't know how to spell.
Moreover, get this through your head:
The current slang for dough is *bread*.

14

What is the opposite of *penny*?
I'm sorry, but there isn't any —
Unless you count the change, I guess,
Of someone who is *penniless*.

When people flip a penny, its
Two *sides*, of course, are opposites.

I'll flip one now. Go on and choose:
Which is it, heads or tails? You lose.

15

The opposite of *squash*? Offhand,
I'd say that it might be *expand*,
Enlarge, uncrumple, or *inflate*.

However, on a dinner plate
With yellow vegetables and green,
The opposite of squash is *bean*.

16

What is the opposite of *actor*?
The answer's very simple: *tractor*.
I said that just because it rhymes,
As lazy poets do at times.

However, to be more exact,
An actor's one who likes to act
King Lear in some unlikely plot,
Pretending to be what he's not.

The opposite of *actor*, friend,
Is *someone who does not pretend*,
But is *himself*, like you and me.
I'm Romeo. Who might you be?

17

There's more than one way to be right
About the opposite of *white*,
And those who merely answer *black*
Are very, very single-track.
They make one want to scream, "I beg
Your pardon, but within an egg
(A fact known to the simplest folk)
The opposite of white is *yolk!*"

18

The opposite of *doughnut?* Wait
A minute while I meditate.

This isn't easy. Ah, I've found it!
A cookie with a hole around it.

19

Because what's *present* doesn't last,
The opposite of it is *past*.
Or if you choose to look ahead,
Future's the opposite instead.
Or look around to see what's here,
And *absent* things will not appear.
There's one more opposite of *present*
That's really almost too unpleasant:
It is *when someone takes away*
Something with which you like to play.

20

What is the opposite of *hat*?
It isn't hard to answer that.
It's *shoes*, for shoes and hat together
Protect our two extremes from weather.

Between these two extremes there lies
A middle, which you would be wise
To clothe as well, or you'll be chilly
And run the risk of looking silly.

21

The opposites of *earth* are two,
And which to choose is up to you.
One opposite is called *the sky,*
And that's where larks and swallows fly;
But angels, there, are few if any,
Whereas in *heaven* there are many.
Well, which word are you voting for?
Do birds or angels please you more?
It's very plain that you are loath
To choose. All right, we'll keep them both.

22

The opposite of a *cloud* could be
A white reflection in the sea,

Or *a huge blueness in the air,*
Caused by a cloud's not being there.

23

Not to have any *hair* is called
Hairlessness, or being *bald*.
It is a fine thing to be hairy,
Yet it's not always necessary.
Bald heads on men are very fine,
Particularly if they shine,
And who conceivably could wish
To see a hairy frog or fish?

Some creatures, though, do well to wear
A normal covering of hair.
I don't think I should care to know
Those hairless dogs of Mexico
Who ramble naked out of doors
And must be patted on their pores.

24

What is the opposite of *Cupid*?
If you don't know, you're pretty stupid.
It's *someone with a crossbow who*
Delights in shooting darts at you.
Not with the kind intention of
Persuading you to fall in love,
But to be mean, and make you shout,
"I hate you," "Ouch," and "Cut it out."

25

What is the opposite of a *shoe*?
Either the *right* or *left* will do,
Depending on which one you've got.
The question's foolish, is it not?

26

What is the opposite of *fleet*?
Someone who's *slow* and drags his feet.

Another's an *armada* that'll
Engage the first fleet in a battle.

What is the opposite of *July*?
That's hard to answer, but I'll try.
In San Francisco and Quebec,
Duluth, Big Forks, Mamaroneck,
And every other city here
In the upper Western Hemisphere,
July can be extremely hot;
But far to southward it is not.
The month can be extremely chill
In Paraguay or in Brazil,
And furthermore, July can mean a
Blizzard or so in Argentina.
These unexpected facts are why
The opposite of July's *July*.

28

What is the opposite of *bat*?
It's easy enough to answer that.
A bat sleeps upside down in trees,
Whereas a *horse,* with equal ease,
Can sleep while upright in his stall.

Another answer might be *ball.*

29

The opposite of *well* is *sick*.

Another answer's *to be quick*
And tell what you have got to tell,
Without a lot of "Well ... well ... well ..."

30

The opposite of *tiller*? Well,
It's *when some farmer in the dell*
Has grown so lazy that by now
He lacks the energy to plow.

A *bowsprit* also comes to mind,
Since, like a tiller, it's a kind
Of stick, and since on sailing craft
The bowsprit's fore, the tiller aft.

I also think of *butter, brads,*
Shoe polish, cannon, shoulder pads,
Daisies, and *stock exchange,* and *goat,*
Since none of these can steer a boat.

31

The opposite of *fast* is *loose*,
And if you doubt it you're a goose.
"Nonsense!" you cry. "As you should know,
The opposite of fast is *slow*."
Well, let's not quarrel: have a chair
And see what's on the bill of fare.

We should agree on this at least:
The opposite of fast is *feast*.

What is the opposite of a *prince*?
A *frog* must be the answer, since,
As all good fairy stories tell,
When some witch says a magic spell,
Causing the prince to be disguised
So that he won't be recognized,
He always ends up green and sad
And sitting on a lily pad.

33

The opposite of a *king*, I'm sure,
Is someone humble and obscure —
A *peasant,* or some *wretched soul*
Who begs through life with staff and bowl.

Another opposite's the *queen,*
If she is quarrelsome and mean.

34

The opposite of *spit*, I'd say,
Would be *a narrow cove or bay.*

(There is another sense of *spit*,
But I refuse to think of it.
It stands opposed to *all refined
And decent instincts of mankind!*)

35

What is the opposite of *ball*?
It's *meteor*. Though meteors fall
As balls do, and like balls are round,
And though they sometimes hit the ground,
They don't know how to bounce or roll
And merely make a dreadful hole.

36

The opposite of *trunk* could be
The taproot of a cedar tree.
In terms of elephants, however,
The answer *tail* is rather clever.

Another answer is *when all*
Your things are tied up in a ball
And carried on your head, for lack
Of anything in which to pack.

37

The opposite of *post*, were you
On horseback, would be *black and blue;*

Another answer is *to fail*
To put your letters in the mail.

38

What is the opposite of *mirror*?
The answer hardly could be clearer:
It's *anything which, on inspection,*
Is not all full of your reflection.

For instance, it would be no use
To brush your hair before a moose,
Or try a raincoat on for size
While looking at a swarm of flies.

39

The opposite of *opposite*?
That's much too difficult. I quit.

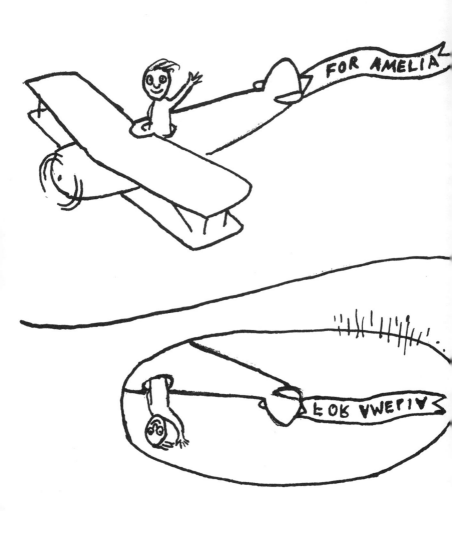

and…

MORE
OPPOSITES

1

The opposite of *duck* is *drake*.
Remember that, for heaven's sake!
One's female, and the other's male.
In writing to a *drake*, don't fail
To start your letter off, "Dear Sir."
"Dear Madam" is what *ducks* prefer.

Mrs. Millard K. Mallard
The Pond
Cummington

In snowball fights, the opposite
Of *duck*, of course, is *getting hit*.

2

The opposite of *doctor*? Well,
That's not so very hard to tell.
A *doctor*'s nice, and when you're ill
He makes you better with a pill.
Then what's his opposite? Don't be thick!
It's *anyone who makes you sick*.

3

What is the opposite of *baby*?
The answer is a *grown-up*, maybe.

4

What is the opposite of *pillow*?
The answer, child, is *armadillo*.
"Oh, don't talk nonsense!" you protest.
However, if you tried to rest
Your head upon the creature, you
Would find that what I say is true.
It isn't soft. From head to tail
It wears a scratchy coat of mail.
And furthermore, it won't hold still
Upon a bed, as pillows will,
But squirms, and jumps at every chance
To run away and eat some ants.

So there! Admit that I was right,
Or else we'll have a *pillow fight*.

5

The opposite of *tar* is *rat*.
If you don't see the sense of that,
Just spell *tar* backwards, and you will.
And there's another reason still:
Though *rats* desert a sinking ship,
A *tar*, with stiffened upper lip,
Will man the bilge-pumps like a sport
And bring the vessel into port.

6

The opposite of *sheep*, I think,
Is when you cannot sleep a wink
And find that you're not counting rams
And ewes and little jumping lambs
But countless *vultures* flocking by
With bony head and searching eye,
Each giving you a sidewise glare
To let you know it knows you're there.

7

How often travelers who mean
To tell us of some cave they've seen
Fall mute, forgetting how to use
Two dreadful words which they confuse!
The word *stalactite* is the first;
Stalagmite means the same, reversed.
Though both these things are formed in time
By dripping carbonate of lime,
Stalactites *hang*, while from beneath,
Stalagmites *rise* like lower teeth.

Can you remember that? You'll find
That you can fix those facts in mind
If you will frequently repeat,
While strolling down the village street
Or waiting for a bus to town,
"Stalagmites up! Stalactites down!"

Take care, though, not to be too loud,
Or you may draw a curious crowd.

8

An *omen* is a sign of some
Occurrence that is *yet to come*,
As when a star, by tumbling down,
Warns that a king will lose his crown.

A *clue*, by contrast, is a sign
By means of which we can divine
What has already taken place —
As when, to cite a common case,
A fish is missing from a platter,
And the cat looks a little fatter.

9

What is the opposite of *road*?
I'd say the answer is *abode*.
"What's an abode?" you ask. I'd say
It's ground that doesn't lead away —
Some patch of earth where you *abide*
Because it makes you satisfied.

Abodes don't take you anywhere,
Because you are already there.

10

The opposite of *"Gee!"* is some
Reaction that is bored and glum,
Like *saying "Big deal" with a shrug*,
Or *staring mutely at the rug.*

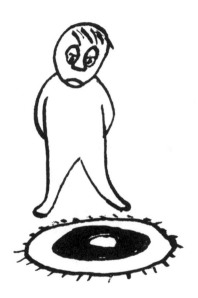

When *"Gee!"* is spoken to a horse,
It bids him take a right-hand course.
Conversely, *"Haw!"* is how to say
"Turn left" and make a horse obey.

"But will a SEA-horse," you inquire,
"Turn *gee* or *haw* as you desire,
Or must you speak of *starboard* and
Of *port* to make him understand?"

How foolish such a question is!
Don't interrupt me, please. *Gee whiz!*

11

The opposite of *kite*, I'd say,
Is *yo-yo*. On a breezy day
You take your *kite* and let it *rise*
Upon its string into the skies,
And then you pull it *down* with ease
(Unless it crashes in the trees).
A *yo-yo*, though, drops *down*, and then
You quickly bring it *up* again
By pulling deftly on its string
(If you can work the blasted thing).

12

When ships send out an *S.O.S.*
It means that they are in distress.
Is there an opposite sort of call
Which means "There's nothing wrong at all"?
Of course not. Ships would think it sappy
To send us word that they are happy.
If you hear *nothing* from a liner,
It means that things could not be finer.

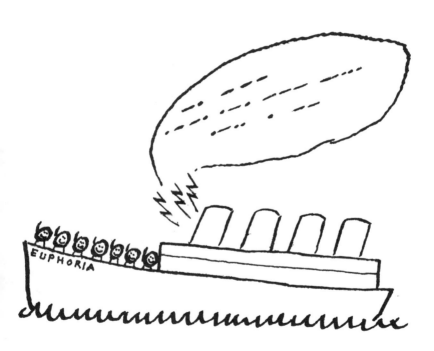

13

When some poor thirsty nomad sees
A far-off fountain fringed with trees
And, making for the spot in haste
Across the blazing desert waste,
Finds that his vision had no basis,
That is the opposite of *oasis*.
What do we call such sad confusion?
Mirage, or *optical illusion*.

Another opposite might be
A sandy islet in the sea.

14

The opposite of *robber*? Come,
You know the answer. Don't be dumb!
While robbers *take things* for a living,
Philanthropists are fond of *giving.*
"And yet," you say, "that's not quite true;
Philanthropists are takers, too,
And often have been very greedy
Before they thought to help the needy."

Well, let's be obvious, then: the op-
Posite of *robber* is a *cop.*

15

The opposite of *less* is *more*.
What's better? Which one are you for?
My question may seem simple, but
The catch is — more or less of *what*?

"Let's have more everything!" you cry.
Well, after we have had more pie,
More pickles, and more layer cake,
I think we'll want *less stomach-ache*.

The best thing's to avoid excess.
Try to be temperate, more or less.

16

An *echo*'s opposite is the *cry*
To which the echo makes reply.
Of course I do not mean to claim
That what they say is not the same.
If one of them calls out "Good day"
Or "Who are you?" or "Hip, hooray"
Or "Robert has an ugly hat,"
The other says exactly that.
But still they're opposites. Know why?
A cry is *bold*; an echo's *shy*,
And though it loves to shout yoo-hoo,
It won't until it hears from you.

17

What is the opposite of *root*?
It's *stem and branch and leaf and fruit* —
All of a plant that we can see.
Another answer, possibly,
Is *when a truffle-hunter's pig*
Has grown too proud to sniff and dig,
And stands there with his snout in air.
(Such happenings are very rare.)

18

A *dragon* is a wingèd snake
Who's always fierce and wide awake
And squats in front of caves which hold
Enormous bags and chests of gold.
If you approach, he bares his nails
And roars at you, and then exhales
Fire, smoke, and sulphur — all of which
Dissuade you from becoming rich.

A dragon's opposite is a *goose*,
A bird who likes to be of use
And who (if of a special breed)
Will give you all you really need
By laying for you every day
A golden egg (or so they say).

19

The opposite of *stunt*? You're right!
It's *making someone grow in height*
By feeding him nutritious bran
Till he's a large and smiling man.
Another answer is *when you*
Do something not too hard to do,
Some act that doesn't call for nerve
And isn't thrilling to observe,
Like sipping from a water glass
Or merely lying on the grass.

20

The opposite of *so-and-so*
Is *anyone whose name you know*,

Or *someone good* who would not take
Your skateboard or your piece of cake,
Making you tell him, with a thwack,
"You so-and-so! I want that back!"

21

The opposite of *punch*, I think,
Might be some sort of *fruitless drink*,
Unless we say that *punch* means *hit*,
In which event the opposite
Is *counter-punch* or *shadow-box*.
Or if we think of *punching clocks*,
I guess the opposite of *punch*
Is *always to be out to lunch*.

What if we capitalize the P?
Judy's the answer then, since she
And *Punch*, although they chose to marry,
Are each the other's adversary —
Each having, ever since they wed,
Pounded the other on the head.

How many things we've thought of! Whew!
I'm getting punchy. That will do.

22

A *spell* is something you are under
When put to sleep, or filled with wonder.
The opposite of *spell*, I guess,
Is *normal waking consciousness*,
In which you're not enthralled or sleepy,
And things are only *fairly* creepy.

Another answer could be *writing*
"*Recieve*," "*Occassional*," and "*fiteing*,"
"*Emporer*," "*mackeral*," and "*snaiks*,"
And other horribel mistaiks.

23

The opposite of *hot*, we know,
Is *icy cold* or *ten below*.
Some other answers to the question
Are *leaky buckets*, *indigestion*,
E-minus, or a *granny knot*,
Since all those things are *not so hot*.

24

The opposite of *moth*? It's *moth*!
One kind is fond of chewing cloth
And biting holes in woolen hats
And coats and dresses and cravats.

However, it's another story
With a nice moth called *Bombyx Mori*,
Who, when it is of tender age
And passing through the larval stage,
Sits munching in a mulberry tree
And spinning silk for you and me —
Of which we make, of course, cravats
As well as dresses, coats, and hats.

25

The opposite of *top*, in case
You haven't heard, is *bottom*, *base*,
Foundation, *underside*, or *foot*.
I also think of *chimney soot*
And *mattresses* and *margarine*,
Since none of those is fun to spin.

When you are playing on a harp,
The opposite of *flat* is *sharp*,
And both sound very good if they
Are what the music says to play.
But when you think it's time to stop
And drink a bit of soda pop,
How bad the thought of flatness is!
A soda should be *full of fizz*.

27

Gray is the opposite of *blue*,
Or was in 1862.

At present, *blue* means *sad and tearful*,
And so its opposite is *cheerful*.

28

What is the opposite of *chew*?
It's *wolf*, which you must never do.
A wolf is said to *wolf* his food,
Because he gulps it down unchewed.
If you must imitate a beast,
Then let it be the cow, at least,
Who eats in such a placid way
And never hurries through her hay.

The cow, however, has a trait
Which there's no need to imitate.
Don't go too far! Don't overdo it!
Chew what you eat, but don't *re*-chew it.
I fear you'd be a social dud
If you were seen to have a *cud*.

29

What is the opposite of a *U*?
An *arch* to knock croquet balls through,
Using a mallet which could be
Described as an inverted *T*.

But how can you invert an *O*?
It's round on top and round below.
It looks as though a croquet ball
May have no opposite at all.

30

I wonder if you've ever seen a
Willow sheltering a *hyena*?
Nowhere in nature can be found
An opposition more profound:
A sad tree weeping inconsolably!
A wild beast laughing uncontrollably!

31

The opposite of *pluck*, my dear,
Is *being overcome by fear.*
(I've thought of one more opposite,
But I don't think I'll mention it,
Since, frankly, I have never heard
Of *adding feathers to a bird.*)

32

The opposite of *sound*? Well, that's
When someone's *ill*, or *wrong*, or *bats*,
Or when some firm is *deep in debt*.
Another answer's *what you get*
By strumming cobwebs with a feather
Or banging powder puffs together.

33

What is the opposite of *Missouri*?
The answer's *California*, surely.
Missouri folk are *doubters* who
Won't take your word for two plus two
Until they add them up, by heck,
And then they like to double-check.

But people on our Western Coast
Believe in everything, almost.
The Californians think, I'm told,
That every river's full of gold,

That stars give good advice to men
On what they ought to do, and when,
And that we all had former lives
As Pharaohs or as Pharaohs' wives.

That's how those states are opposite.
I may exaggerate a bit,
But I have told you what we say
In *Massachusetts*, anyway.

34

The opposite of *stop* is *go*,
But sometimes one does both, you know.
We've come at last, by pleasant stages,
To where there are no further pages,
And since our book is at an end,
I'll *stop*. And *go*. Farewell, my friend.

But wait...

here's...

A FEW
DIFFERENCES

1

Dawn is a thing that poets write
Verses about till late at night.
At *daybreak*, when the poets' eyes
Are closed in sleep, their neighbors rise
And put the coffee on to perk
And drink it, and go off to work.

2

An *owl* is like a *cat* because
Both pounce on rodents with their claws,
And look about the same in size,
And pierce the dark with round, bright eyes.
But cats are *beasts*, whereas an owl
Has wings, of course, and is a *fowl*.
An *owl* can fly up into trees
And then swoop down again with ease;
But when a *cat* is on a limb
A sudden dread can madden him
And make him howl, and grow still madder,
Until some person brings a ladder.

3

You don't confuse a *cake of soap*
With *other sorts of cake*, I hope.
Were you to eat a helping of
Camay, or *Ivory*, or *Dove*,
I think you'd have digestive troubles
Caused by a stomach full of bubbles.

How horrible! But the reverse
Confusion might be even worse.
Be careful, if you please: I'd rather
Not see you bathe in *mocha* lather,
Or watch as you shampoo your head
With *angel food* or *gingerbread*.

4

How is a *room* unlike a *moor*?
They're not the same, you may be sure.
A *room* has walls, a *moor* does not.
Inquire of any honest Scot
And he will say, I have no doubt,
That one's indoors and one is out.
A *room*, then, fits inside a dwelling;
A *moor* is its reverse in spelling,
And has such wild outdoorish weather,
Such rocks, such miles and miles of heather
All full of flocks of drumming grouse,
You wouldn't have one in the house.

5

In what way do your two lips differ?
The *upper one* is somewhat stiffer,
And useful for expressing pluck
When faced with danger or ill-luck.

The *lower one's* for sticking out
When there's a need to sulk and pout.

6

The kindly barber trims your *nape*,
Then gives your hair a pleasing shape,
And lastly, with his busy shears,
Snips carefully around your ears.
How nice he is! But what if you
Refused to pay when he was through?
I think he'd take you by the *scruff*
And shake you, and be pretty rough.

7

A *jester* differs from a *dunce*
In ways that one can state at once:
Each of them is a kind of fool,
One at the court, and one at school,
And both are given funny caps:
But one of them is bright, perhaps.